Sharks!

By
Rhonda Lucas Donald
and
Kathleen W. Kranking

NEW YORK • TORONTO • LONDON • AUCKLAND • SYDNEY
MEXICO CITY • NEW DELHI • HONG KONG

Scholastic Inc. grants teachers permission to photocopy the reproducible pages from this book for classroom use. No other part of this publication may be reproduced in whole or in part, or stored in a retrieval system, or transmitted in any form or by any means, electronic, mechanical, photocopying, recording, or otherwise, without written permission of the publisher. For information regarding permission, write to Scholastic Inc., 555 Broadway, New York, NY 10012.

Cover and poster design by Norma Ortiz
Cover photo of sandbar shark © David B. Fleetham/Innerspace Visions
Interior design by Solutions by Design, Inc.
Interior illustrations by Patricia J. Wynne
Photo research by Sarah Longacre

ISBN: 0-439-09837-8

Copyright © 2001 by Rhonda Lucas Donald and Kathleen W. Kranking
All rights reserved. Printed in the U.S.A.

Contents

How to Use This Book 4

Background Information 5

Student Activities 9

    Sharks and Minnows (Movement) 9

    Sharks, Big and Small (Math, Science) 9

  🦈 **Swimmin' Sharks Are We** (Art, Music, Science) 10

  🦈 **What Sharp Teeth…** (Critical Thinking, Language Arts, Art) 11

    Like Oil and Water (Critical Thinking, Science) 11

  🦈 **A Nose for Hunting** (Science) 12

    Shark Signals (Science) 12

  🦈 **The Strangest Names** (Language Arts, Art, Science) 13

    Where's the Fish Gone, Wobbegong? (Art, Science) 13

  🦈 **Sharks on the Move** (Mapping, Math, Science) 14

  🦈 **Make a Mermaid's Purse** (Art, Science) 15

    Shark Poems (Language Arts, Science, Art) 16

  🦈 **Troubled Waters** (Science, Critical Thinking, Art) 17

  🦈 **Scientist for a Day** (Math) 17

    Buddies or Bothers? (Science, Art) 17

    Save the Sharks Campaign (Language Arts, Science, Art) 18

    Teaching With the "Super Sharks!" Poster (Science, Math, Art) 19

  🦈 **The Toothy Times** (Language Arts, Math, Science) 19

Student Reproducible Pages 20

Shark Resources 32

Poster: "Super Sharks!" (bound in the center of the book)

  🦈 = Activities with student reproducibles

How to Use This Book

Welcome to Sharks!

The mention of sharks may bring shrieks from your students. Children may be fascinated with what they think are giant man-eaters, but they will become even more enthralled when they learn the truth about sharks. This in-depth resource provides background information, creative cross-curricular activities, hands-on reproducibles, and a giant, colorful poster—everything you need for a super theme unit on sharks. Once children have distinguished the facts from the myths, they'll have a better understanding and deeper appreciation for these spectacular creatures. Before you dive into learning about sharks, here are few helpful tips for using this book.

1. Separate facts from myths.

Before beginning your shark studies, ask kids to write down three things they know about sharks. Then ask children how they feel about sharks. What words would they use to describe these creatures? Have students keep their lists and descriptions until you complete the unit. At the end of your shark unit, kids can review their lists to see which of their "facts" were true and which were myths. They can also compare how they felt about sharks before and after studying them.

2. Choose activities that meet your students' needs and interests.

Browse through the activities, and select those that connect with your students' interests and learning styles as well as the content areas you would like to teach. Feel free to adapt the activities or develop spin-off projects to meet the needs of your students.

3. Share "fishy" stories.

Be sure to have lots of fiction and nonfiction books on hand to pique students' interest in sharks. You can even set aside a time each day for shark reading—call it "The Reading Frenzy!" Challenge your students to "gobble up" shark books the way sharks gobble up fish! Throughout the activities in this book, you'll find Book Breaks—brief reviews of shark books as well as suggested activities. Additional resources are suggested on page 32.

4. Teach with the "Super Sharks!" poster.

Show students the poster and ask them which of the fish are sharks. They will probably recognize the great white shark and the hammerhead. But they may be surprised to learn that the whale shark, leopard shark, and wobbegong are also sharks. Talk about the similarities and differences between the species on the poster. Ask children how they think some of the creatures got their names. Then read the text aloud. This is a great way to spark students' interest and encourage them to find out more about the many different kinds of sharks. Display the poster in a science learning center along with books and magazines about sharks.

5. Saving Sharks

As your class will learn, people's misconceptions about sharks have given these creatures a bad reputation. Students may be surprised to learn that people are much more dangerous to sharks than sharks are to people. Many shark species are declining rapidly, and rules against catching certain types of sharks are now being enforced in some places. But some people are reluctant to help animals they consider "bad." Your students can help dispel the myths surrounding sharks by educating others about these fascinating fish. Put the crafts, poems, and other materials your students generate from the activities to good use. Display their finished work in your school, local library, or elsewhere to spread the word that sharks are interesting creatures that need our help.

Background Information

The Scoop on Sharks

Shark—the word conjures up various frightening images: a sleek fin cutting ominously through the water, sharp teeth snapping, the struggles of a hapless victim. Portrayals of sharks in movies and literature have unfortunately given all sharks a bad rap. Just about everyone is familiar with dangerous species such as the great white shark, tiger shark, and bull shark. But these are just a few of the approximately 375 species in the shark family, most of which don't fit the image portrayed by the movie *Jaws*. Sharks can be as gentle as the gigantic whale shark, as small as the banana-sized dwarf dogshark, or as bizarre as the bottom-dwelling wobbegong. Some are as flat as a pancake, others are covered with fancy fringes, and a few even glow in the dark! So if you thought you already knew all about sharks, it may be time for a second look.

Sharks inhabit the oceans worldwide, from tropical waters to polar regions. Though their size varies from about $6\frac{1}{2}$ inches to more than 40 feet, many are less than 3 feet long. Sharks first appeared in ancient seas about 400 million years ago, long before dinosaurs existed.

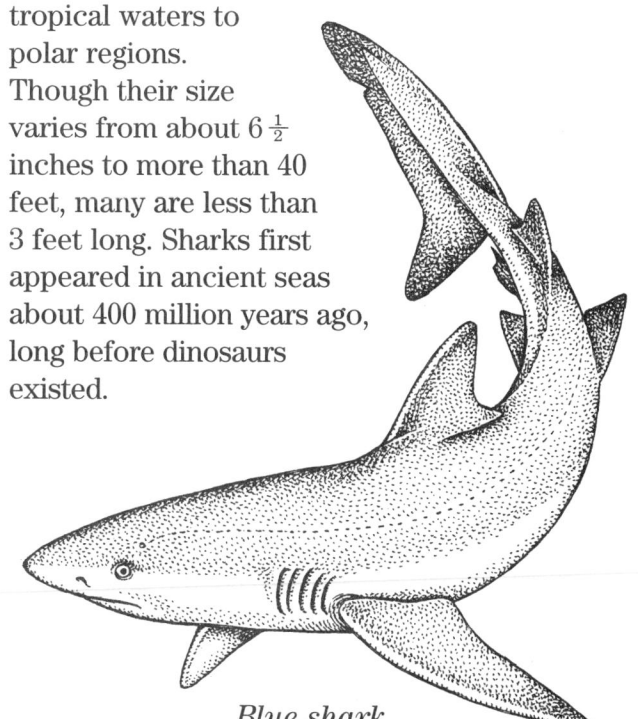

Blue shark

> The megalodon shark, which lived at least five million years ago, was the length of two school buses and had 6-inch teeth!

Though some sharks do attack and kill people, their reputation as bloodthirsty killers has been greatly exaggerated. Each year sharks attack 50 to 75 people worldwide; five to ten of those attacks result in death. Some of these attacks may occur because the sharks mistake humans for seals or fish, their usual prey.

Inside and Out

Sharks are unique among fish in that they have no bones. Instead, their skeleton is made of rubbery cartilage. This is also true of their cartilaginous cousins—the skates, rays, and chimaeras. Sharks differ from bony fish in a few other ways, too. For one thing, they have gill slits instead of the gill covers of bony fish. As a shark breathes, water comes in through its mouth, flows over its gills, and goes back out through the shark's gill slits. As the water passes over the gills, oxygen is absorbed into the shark's body. Most sharks have five gill slits.

All fish have scales, right? Not sharks. While the skin of bony fish is covered with scales, shark skin is covered with denticles—toothlike projections that give their skin its rough texture. Another difference between sharks and bony fish is that bony fish have a gas-filled sac called a swim bladder that they use to control their buoyancy. Though sharks have no swim bladder, they do have oil-filled livers that help reduce their weight in the water. However, most sharks will sink if they stop swimming.

Looking a Shark in the Mouth

You might say sharks have more than a mouthful of teeth. That's because a shark may have up to 3,000 teeth in its mouth at one time! A shark's teeth are arranged in rows—as many as 20 in some species. The shark uses the teeth in the first row or two. Subsequent rows contain replacement teeth, which move forward when primary teeth break or fall out. The teeth are embedded in the shark's gums rather than attached to its jaws. During its life a shark produces thousands of teeth. In some species, the teeth are replaced individually; in others they may be replaced a row at a time.

> A shark may use more than 20,000 teeth in its lifetime!

Great white shark

Sharks' teeth are shaped differently, according to what they eat. Predatory sharks that eat large prey have big, razor-sharp teeth for cutting and tearing a meal into bite-sized pieces. Fish-eating sharks have long, thin teeth for grasping their slippery, wiggily prey. Bottom-dwelling sharks that eat crustaceans have flattened teeth for crushing shells. And filter feeders, such as basking sharks and whale sharks, don't use their teeth for eating at all. They filter food from the water using rows of bristles called gill rakers.

What's on the Menu?

Of course, different kinds of sharks eat different kinds of foods. But in general, there aren't too many creatures that are safe from becoming a snack for a hungry shark. Shark meals can include plankton, crabs, mussels, sea urchins, fish, shrimp, lobsters, rays, squid, jellyfish, seals, seabirds, sea turtles, and other sharks. Even things like tin cans and plastic bags have been found in the stomachs of bigger sharks.

Making Sense of It All

Sharks were once known as "swimming noses" because of their excellent sense of smell. In fact, the part of a shark's brain that controls the sense of smell is twice as large as the rest. Sharks can detect odors in the water from almost a mile away! Unlike many other animals, they use their nostrils only for smelling, never for breathing.

> Sharks can detect one drop of blood in 25 gallons of water.

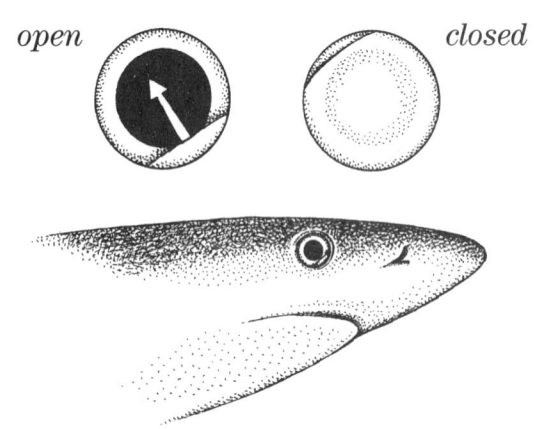

Nictitating membranes

Sharks also have good eyesight, and they can even see well in dim light, as cats can. To protect their eyes, sharks have special eyelids called nictitating membranes. These membranes automatically cover a shark's eyes when it

attacks, protecting them from possible injury by struggling prey. Sharks pick up sounds from the water using inner ears, rather than external ears like people. Sounds enter a shark's ears through two small pores on top of its head.

When it comes to getting information about their surroundings, sharks have a couple of "bonus" senses. One is called a lateral line system, which consists of a series of canals along the sides of a shark's body and head. These canals are made up of tiny, jelly-filled pores, and beneath them are cells with sensitive hairs. The shark uses its lateral line system to detect vibrations in the water, such as those made by moving prey.

The shark's other bonus sense comes from sensory pores called ampullae of Lorenzini, which are filled with jelly and connect to sensitive nerves. Located around the shark's snout, they detect the weak electrical signals emitted by prey.

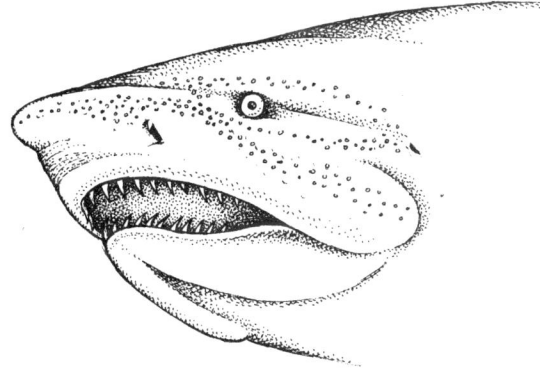

Ampullae of Lorenzini

Scientists think that sharks have a built-in compass to help them find their way around the ocean. Some sharks migrate hundreds of miles. Their ability to sense changes in their own electrical field in relation to the earth's magnetic field enables them to maintain a sense of direction.

> The mako shark is probably the fastest fish—swimming at more than 60 miles per hour!

Getting Around

Sharks' streamlined bodies, particularly their tails and fins, are built to help them cruise through the ocean efficiently. They move their tails from side to side to propel themselves, while using their pectoral (side) fins for balance. By slightly changing the angle of the fins, they can swim up, down, left, or right. The pectoral fins are also used for braking. Sharks cannot, however, swim backward, nor can they hover. Sharks that live on the sea floor use their pectoral fins for crawling.

Most smaller sharks have fairly flexible bodies, enabling them to make quick twists and turns when chasing prey. Larger sharks such as the great white, however, are not able to bend their bulky bodies as much. They rely on the element of surprise and on bursts of speed to get a meal.

Hatching From Eggs

When sharks mate, the female's eggs are fertilized inside her body. This method

> The egg cases of some sharks are called "mermaid's purses."

differs from that of bony fish, which simply shed their sperm and eggs into the water. After mating takes place, young sharks develop in a variety of ways. In oviparous sharks, the young hatch from eggs laid outside the mother's body, like birds. The eggs are covered with a leathery case that is soft at first but hardens in the seawater. Depending on the kind of shark that laid them, egg cases may have curly tendrils that help anchor them to seaweed, or they may be shaped in such a way that they can wedge between rock crevices, safe from predators.

The developing shark embryo may stay for months inside the egg case, where it is nourished by a large yolk sac. Once it has used up all of its yolk sac, the shark hatches and swims away on its own.

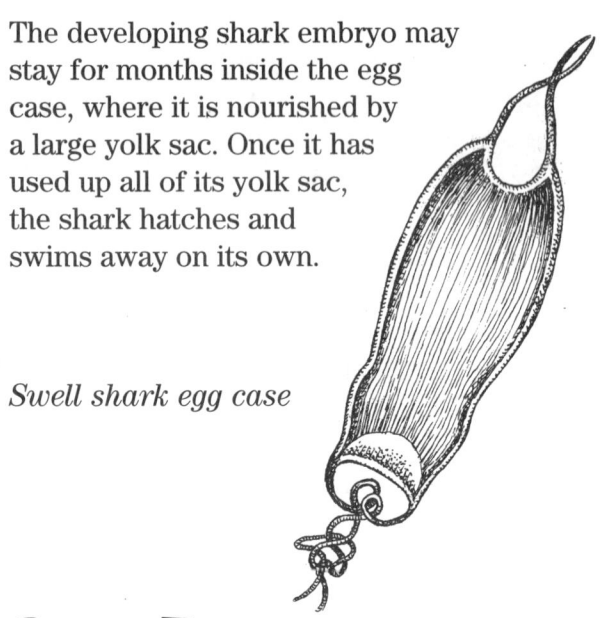

Swell shark egg case

Born Free

Rather than lay eggs, most sharks give birth to live young. In ovoviviparous sharks, the shark embryos develop in a yolky egg inside the mother's body. They hatch within the body, continue to develop, and are later "reborn." In viviparous sharks, the embryos also develop inside the body, getting nourishment through a placenta until they are born. At that time they swim off, able to fend for themselves. Some sharks have a nine-month gestation period, as humans do, but others may gestate as long as two years.

Bad News for Sharks

Despite their dangerous reputation, sharks have much more to fear from people than do people from sharks. Sharks face a big threat worldwide from overfishing. People have found ways to use almost every part of a shark's body. They use the teeth for jewelry and the skin to make leather. They make soup from the fins and eat the flesh. Oil from shark livers is used in medicines and cosmetics. Sharks' jaws, especially from large sharks, are sold as souvenirs. Many sharks are killed for sport. And many more are killed accidentally in nets meant for other types of fish. Since sharks have a fairly low rate of reproduction, their numbers may never recover if too many are killed. Sharks also face declines in their population due to habitat destruction or degradation.

There is some good news, however. People are becoming aware of the problems sharks face, and they are making an effort to protect them. In some places the hunting of sharks has been restricted or even banned completely.

And here's some more good news: As people learn about sharks, they come to admire them rather than fear them. Now that many aquariums house various types of sharks, people have the chance to see these animals for what they really are: beautiful, graceful creatures that deserve not only our respect but also our fascination.

The jaws of a great white shark can be almost 2 feet wide!

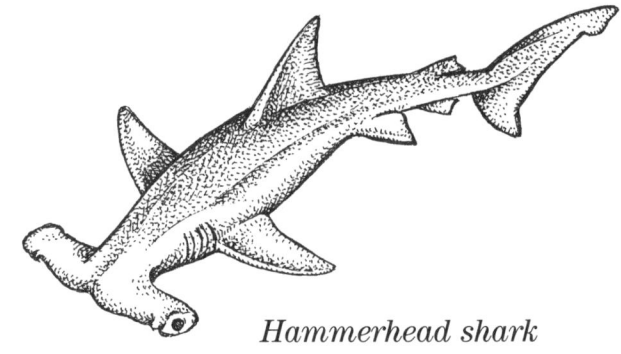

Hammerhead shark

Student Activities

Sharks and Minnows
(Movement)

Students play an active shark game.

A classic game of Sharks and Minnows will rev kids up to learn about sharks. Here's how to play, either outdoors or in a gymnasium.

- Mark off the boundaries of a large rectangular area for kids to run around in.

- Ask for a student volunteer to be the shark. Explain that he or she must stay inside the boundary lines. The rest of the kids are minnows. They gather at one end of the rectangle, outside the boundary.

- When you say "go," the minnows run to the other side of the playing area, trying to avoid the shark. Once they cross the other end line, they are safe. But if the shark tags them, they too become sharks and must stay inside the boundary.

- Continue playing until only one minnow remains. He or she becomes the shark for the next round.

Sharks, Big and Small
(Math, Science)

Students compare their own heights to the sizes of various sharks.

How do your students measure up to sharks? Find out by drawing several sharks to scale. You can use sidewalk chalk to draw outdoors or long sheets of craft paper to draw indoors. Begin by drawing a shark shape that is 12 feet long (see sharks at right for reference). Explain that this is the size of a tiger shark. Let kids compare their height with the shark's length. Next, draw a smaller shark, the $3\frac{1}{2}$-foot-long epaulette shark. One of the smallest sharks is the dwarf dogfish, which is only about 6 inches long. Draw its shape as well. Ask children to estimate and then find out how many dwarf dogfishes drawn end to end will fit inside the epaulette shark. (The answer is seven.) Finally, measure off a 40-foot length of string and stretch it out. Explain that this is the length of the giant whale shark. How many students would have to lie head to toe to equal the length of this big fish? (Estimate the average height of students in your class. Then divide 40 feet by the average student height.)

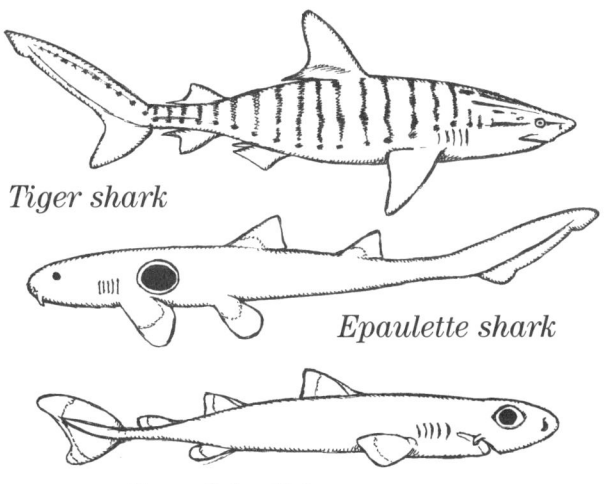

Tiger shark

Epaulette shark

Dwarf dogfish

Note: These illustrations are not drawn to scale.

 *Sharks* by Gail Gibbons (Holiday House, 1992) is a good introduction to sharks that beginning readers can read by themselves. At the end of the book, kids will find an important notice about what to do if they see a shark while swimming. Share this information with your class. Assign them the job of teaching family members or friends about shark safety. To do this, they can make a poster outlining the steps to take if one sees a shark while swimming.

Swimmin' Sharks Are We

(Art, Music, Science)

Students make a shark and sing a shark song.

Have students make their own "swimmin' sharks" to reinforce some characteristics of sharks. The finished sharks can be used as props for the fun shark song on page 20. Give each student a copy of the templates on page 21 and the following supplies:

- pencil, glue, and scissors
- empty paper-towel roll (or one-third of a cardboard wrapping-paper tube)
- fine sandpaper, approximately 11- by 6-inches (large enough to wrap around the cardboard tube)
- 6- by 6-inch square of fine sandpaper (or several smaller scraps)
- 12-inch piece of white rickrack
- 2 movable eyes (or small construction paper circles)

Then show students how to make a swimmin' leopard shark by following these simple directions:

1 Cut a mouth out of one end of the tube, as shown.

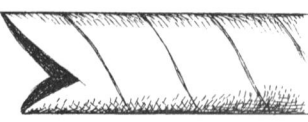

2 Glue the larger piece of sandpaper around the middle of the tube.

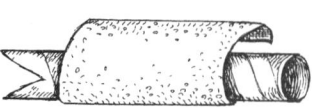

3 Cut out the fin and tail templates on page 21. Trace the templates onto sandpaper, and cut them out. Glue the two halves of the dorsal fin together. Then glue the two halves of the tail together.

4 For the dorsal fin, fold out the bottom edges slightly, as shown, so it will be easy to glue it to the shark. Glue a pectoral fin on each side of the shark, sandpaper side facing up.

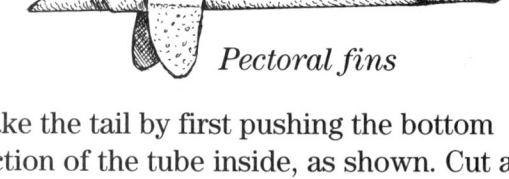

Dorsal fin
Pectoral fins

5 Make the tail by first pushing the bottom section of the tube inside, as shown. Cut a half-inch slit in the top of the tube. Cut a 1-inch slit in the front of the sandpaper tail. Slide the tail slit into the tube slit, and adjust the tail so it stands up properly.

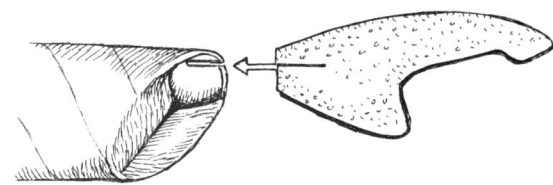

6 Run a line of glue along the inside edges of the mouth, and attach rickrack teeth. Glue a movable eye to each side of the head.

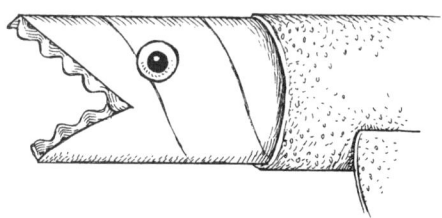

7 Use a black marker to draw the shark's gills and spots.

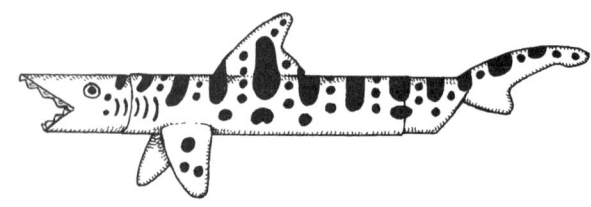

Make copies of the song lyrics on page 20. Sing the song a few times (to the tune of the theme song from the television show *The Addams Family*) until students become familiar with the tune and words. Invite children to sing

along whenever they feel comfortable. Encourage children to use their swimmin' leopard sharks as props while singing the song. If desired, make up specific motions to go with particular parts of the song, such as moving the shark in a swimming motion whenever children sing the line "Swimmin' sharks are we."

What Sharp Teeth...
(Critical Thinking, Language Arts, Art)

Students read clues to discover what different sharks eat.

Students will probably be familiar with the huge, sharp teeth of a great white shark. But did they know that the world's largest sharks have barely any teeth at all? Did they know that other sharks have teeth specially designed to help them eat specific types of prey?

For example, the swell shark has tiny, ridged teeth in the front of its mouth and large, flat teeth in the back that are perfect for crushing shellfish or crustaceans. The long, sharp teeth of the sand tiger shark help it snag and hold on to fish or squid. The whale shark has scarcely any teeth. It captures its food with gill rakers, comblike bristles that trap plankton and strain it from the water as the shark swims. (For more information, see page 6.)

After reviewing information on shark teeth, give each student a copy of the reproducible on page 22. Read through the clues with children. Then help them match each clue to a type of shark by using a process of elimination. When children are finished, invite them to color the illustrations. Finally, review the answers with the class and show children pictures of shark teeth in reference books.

Answers: 1—sand tiger shark, 2—cookie-cutter shark, 3—great white shark, 4—swell shark, 5—sawshark

BOOK BREAK *Chomp: A Book About Sharks* by Melvin Berger (Scholastic, 1999) has tips for helping parents and children read together. Consider letting kids take this book home to share with their families. Send home a brief note to draw family members' attention to the reading tips at the beginning of the book.

Like Oil and Water
(Critical Thinking, Science)

To learn how fish and sharks stay afloat, students observe a simple demonstration with water, oil, and a balloon.

If sea creatures didn't have special adaptations, they might sink rather than float! Bony fish have an air-filled swim bladder that helps keep them afloat, but sharks don't have air bladders. Instead, they have oil-filled livers. How can oily livers help keep sharks afloat? Do this easy demonstration to illustrate. You will need a small, round balloon, a large bowl filled with water, a clear measuring cup, and a quarter cup of oil.

1 Explain that bony fish have swim bladders that are filled with air to keep the fish afloat. To demonstrate how this works, blow up the balloon. Ask what will happen if you place it in water, and then demonstrate. Show what happens if you push the balloon underwater (it will pop back up). Explain that the balloon floats because it is filled with air, and air is lighter than water. Air-filled swim bladders in fish work in the same way.

2 Have students guess how sharks stay afloat even though they don't have swim bladders. Explain that large, very oily livers help them float in a way similar to the swim bladders of fish. To demonstrate, pour a half cup of water into a clear measuring cup. Then pour a quarter cup of oil into the same cup. The oil will float on top because it is lighter than the water.

3 Ask kids which type of "flotation device" seems better. (Air bladders are more effective. Even with the help of their oily livers, many sharks must swim to keep from sinking.)

A Nose for Hunting
(Science)

Students answer questions about sharks as they navigate a maze.

Sharks have a powerful sense of smell. Scientists estimate that some sharks can smell blood from almost a mile away. Review the information about sharks' sense of smell on page 6. Give each child a copy of the reproducible maze on page 23. Have children read the first trivia question and circle on the maze the answer they think is correct. Before moving on to the next question, review the correct answer with children (answers are provided in parentheses following each question below). As children move from one correct answer to the next, they will help the shark "follow its nose" and find its way through the maze.

Shark Trivia Questions

1 Sharks' skin is covered with _____. (denticles)

2 Sharks' _____ are constantly replaced. (teeth)

3 Sharks breathe with _____. (gills)

4 All sharks are carnivores, which means they eat _____. (meat)

5 Sharks are related to _____. (rays)

6 True or false? Sharks are always harmful to people. (False. While it is true that some sharks kill people, the incidence is quite low. Scientists believe that sharks may mistake people for other prey and attack them accidentally. Most sharks shy away from people.)

7 One of the biggest threats to sharks today comes from _____. (people. Sharks are threatened by people who hunt them or unintentionally catch them.)

BOOK BREAK Do your students have lots of questions about sharks? *I Didn't Know That Sharks Keep Losing Their Teeth* by Claire Llewellyn (Cooper Beech, 1998) provides answers to many questions and highlights interesting facts about sharks. For example, sharks existed before dinosaurs, and some sharks glow in the dark! You'll find trivia questions throughout the book, as well as activities and games. Invite children to make up their own shark games based on the artwork in the book.

Shark Signals
(Science)

Students perform a simple experiment with a balloon to simulate how a shark might sense electrical fields.

Sharks have senses that we do not. A shark's lateral line extends up and down the sides of its body. The lateral line has tiny tubes that sense vibrations in the water that may be caused by the movements of other animals. Sharks are also able to detect electrical fields using organs called ampullae of Lorenzini, which are jelly-filled pores connected to sensitive nerves. Scientists believe that sharks can detect very weak electrical fields, including those generated by the bodies of fish and other living things. These special senses help sharks find food and maneuver through dark waters. (For more information, see page 7.)

Help students understand how being able to detect an electrical field might help sharks. Here's how:

1 Pair students up and give each pair a small, blown-up balloon. Blindfold one student in each pair, and have him or her roll up both shirt sleeves.

2 The other student should rub the balloon briskly against his or her own clothes and then slowly wave the balloon close to (but not touching) one of the blindfolded student's arms. Have the blindfolded student guess which arm the balloon was near. The student should be able to tell because hairs on the arm react to the static electricity, letting the student sense its presence.

3 Have partners switch roles.

Note: Rubbing a balloon against clothing creates static electricity, which makes hairs on the arm stand up. This experiment doesn't work in the same way as a shark's ampullae of Lorenzini, but it can give students an idea of how sensing electrical fields might be helpful to a shark.

The Strangest Names
(Language Arts, Art, Science)

Students learn unusual shark names and draw shark pictures.

Some sharks have very unusual names, as this activity shows. Display several shark books for students to refer to as they complete this activity. Give each student a copy of the reproducible on page 24. Have them read the clues and shark names at the bottom of the page. Explain that they should write a shark name beside the clue that best describes that name. (Each name is used only once.) Kids will then have fun creating their own made-up shark names as well.

Answers: 1—hammerhead shark, 2—lantern shark, 3—bonnethead shark, 4—angel shark, 5—goblin shark, 6—zebra shark

Where's the Fish Gone, Wobbegong?
(Art, Science)

Students make a wobbegong shark puppet to play Catch the Fish.

Wobbegongs are very strange-looking sharks! And tasseled wobbegongs may be the weirdest of all. For one thing, their bodies are very flat. This comes in handy for hanging out on the ocean floor, where they blend in with the silt. Their eyes are on top of their head, so they can see even when they are partly buried under silt. And the tasseled wobbegong has whiskery barbels that look like seaweed all around its mouth. These sharks blend into the ocean floor so well that it's very hard to see them. If an unlucky fish gets too close—gulp! The shark sucks it into its wide mouth.

Show children how to make a tasseled wobbegong puppet by following the steps below. Show children the wobbegong on the poster for reference. Children can use the puppets to play a fun game of Catch the Fish (directions on page 14). To make a wobbegong puppet, each child will need:

- tape, scissors, and a hole punch
- 3 thin paper plates
- brown or gray paint
- paintbrushes
- sponge (optional)
- brown or gray yarn
- black marker or paint

1 Fold a thin paper plate in half so that the edges curve in toward each other. Lay the folded plate over the second paper plate so that the ridges line up with each other. (Do not glue the plates together.) Use a hole punch to punch holes through both plates, from one side of the fold to the other. Holes should be about an inch apart and very close to the edge of the plates.

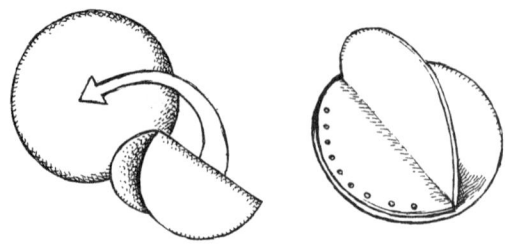

2. Cut fins out of the third plate and tape them to the underside of the unfolded plate.

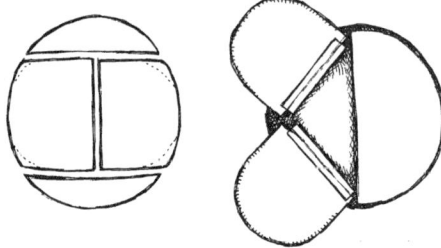

3. Cut a 1-inch by 3-inch strip from the third paper plate. Bend the strip into a U and tape to the underside of the folded plate, about an inch from the fold. The strip should be slack enough for a child to fit a thumb through easily.

4. Paint the wobbegong with markers or paint. Sponging several shades of brown or gray paint creates a mottled look very much like the patterns on a real wobbegong. Paint the inside and underside of the mouth gray. Let the paint dry completely.

5. Cut several pieces of yarn about 7 inches long, and use them to tie the top of the wobbegong to the top of the folded mouth. Thread the yarn through both plates and knot. The more pieces of yarn you use, the more tasseled the wobbegong will be.

6. Use a marker or paint to make the wobbegong's eyes on top of its head.

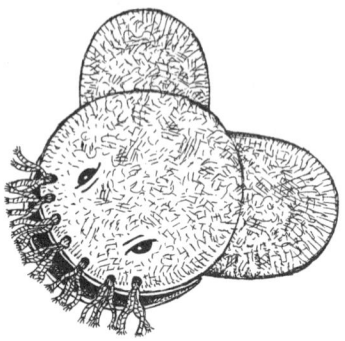

7. Make a fish for the game by cutting a 4-inch fish shape out of a paper plate and coloring it. Punch a hole through the fish's top fin, and tie a 24-inch piece of yarn through it.

To play Catch the Fish, have one student hold the wobbegong puppet on a tabletop. Another student holds the fish by the end of the yarn and dangles it near the wobbegong. When the fish comes close enough, the student operating the wobbegong puppet tries to catch it. Have kids take turns being the wobbegong and the fish.

Sharks on the Move
(Mapping, Math, Science)

Students trace on a map the migration route of a blue shark.

Like many other animals, some sharks migrate long distances at different times of the year. The blue shark is a champion migrator, traveling from waters off the northeast coast of the United States to as far away as Brazil and West Africa. Why do sharks migrate? They migrate in order to find food and have their pups. At certain times of the year, it may be easier for sharks to find prey in different waters, so they follow the food.

Give each student a copy of the reproducible map on page 25. Guide them to use their finger to trace the possible migration

route of a blue shark (the route is shown as a dashed line). Explain that in 1983 a blue shark was tagged off the coast of New York and released. When it was recaptured 17 months later, it was off the coast of Brazil, 3,740 miles away. Then help students answer the question on the map, using these tips.

Show students how to use a string to trace the path of a blue shark from New York to Brazil. Place the string along the dashed line that represents the migration route. Kids can tape the string at various points if they are having difficulty holding it in place. Have kids cut the string so that it is the same length as the migration route. Then demonstrate how to measure the length of string against the mileage scale. The string should be long enough to reach across the mileage scale nearly four times, or 4,000 miles.

Make a Mermaid's Purse
(Art, Science)

Students make a reclosable pouch that looks like a shark egg case with a baby swell shark inside!

Some sharks are born live. After hatching from eggs inside the mother's body, the baby sharks emerge fully developed. Other sharks are born from eggs the mother lays outside her body. Shark eggs don't look like those that birds lay. Some eggs are conical with spiraling edges. Others are oblong cases that attach to ocean vegetation with dangling tendrils. These egg cases are called mermaid's purses. Inside the purse, the baby shark is attached to the egg yolk from which it draws nutrients until it's ready to hatch. (For more information, see pages 7–8.)

In this activity, kids make their own mermaid's purses, complete with a baby swell shark inside! Kids can carry the finished project like a purse or they can tie it to their belt like a pouch. The purse or pouch is handy for carrying pencils, coins, or other small items.

Give each student a copy of the templates on page 26 and the following supplies:

- scissors, pencil, and glue
- 10- by 9-inch piece of tan felt or construction paper (felt is more durable)
- one 2- by 2-inch piece of white construction paper or felt
- one 8-inch piece of string
- four 4-inch pieces of string
- small piece of self-sticking Velcro™
- black marker

Show students how to make a mermaid's purse by following these directions:

1 Cut out the templates on the reproducible page. Trace the templates onto the felt and

cut out the shapes. (On tan felt, trace the baby swell shark once and the mermaid's purse twice. On white felt, trace the yolk template once.)

2 Place one end of the 8-inch string in the middle of one egg case. Glue the felt circle on top to hold the string in place. (The circle represents the egg yolk.)

3 Glue a 4-inch string to each of the points on the same egg case. Then run a line of glue around the outside edge of the egg case, without putting glue between the two points at the top of the case (the end that doesn't curve in). This will be the purse's opening. *Do* put glue over the yarn pieces on each point. Place the other egg case on top, lining up the two halves. (Children may need help with this step.)

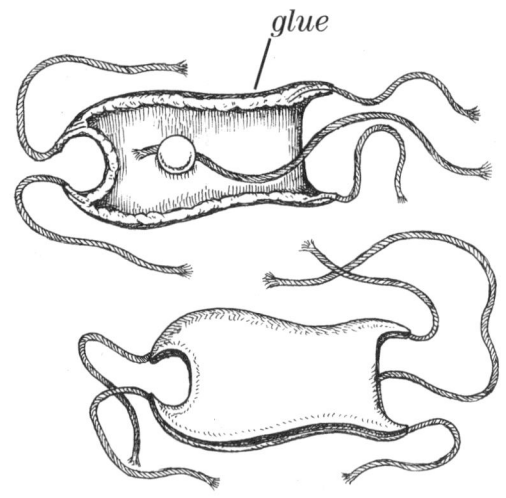

4 Use a marker to draw the shark's eyes and spots.

5 Glue the other end of the 8-inch string to the underside of the baby shark (the side without any spots). After the glue dries, attach Velcro™ pieces to the inside of the purse's opening. Put the baby shark inside and close the purse.

Shark Poems
(Language Arts, Science, Art)

Students write different types of poems using sharks as inspiration.

Sharks are a wonderful topic for all kinds of poems. After children have written their poems, encourage them to add illustrations. Here are a few kinds of poems to try:

Shape poem: The lines of the poem form a shape relevant to the topic of the poem. (For this activity, children could write a poem in the shape of a shark, or even a fin or tooth.) First, encourage children to write a rough draft of the poem. Have them lightly draw an outline of the shape and then write the poem in that shape.

Acrostic poem: Each line of the poem begins with a letter in a word. For example, if the word is *shark*, the first line begins with *s*, the next begins with *h*, and so on. Each line usually consists of just one word, but kids can also write a phrase or sentence that begins with the appropriate letter. Encourage students to use this form to write poems about specific types of sharks.

Shark mobile poem: Invite children to write short poems about sharks. Then have them cut out several simple shark shapes and write the words of the poem on the sharks. They can write one or more words on each shark. Help children punch holes in each shark and string them onto pieces of thread. Suspend the sharks from a coat hanger or wire, positioning them so that they can be read from top to bottom. (This last step will need to be done by a teacher or parent volunteer, with help from the student.)

Motion poem: After children have written shark poems, invite them to make up motions to go with their poems.

Troubled Waters
(Science, Critical Thinking, Art)

Students color an ocean scene and identify the dangers to sharks.

People and industries pose a serious threat to sharks. Fishermen catch millions of sharks every year. But even more die from being accidentally caught on lines and in nets meant to catch other types of fish. Many sharks are killed to make shark fin soup. Just as habitat loss affects other animals, the same is true for sharks. Many shark nurseries are located in areas that are being developed or polluted by people. In addition to the problems generated by humans, young and small sharks are also susceptible to being preyed upon by larger ocean predators.

Your students can help the shark on page 27 negotiate the dangerous waters it's in. Invite children to color the page and then circle the things in the scene that can be harmful to the shark. Ask kids why these things pose a threat, and discuss some of the reasons. Then have kids answer the question, "How would you help sharks?"

Answers: Dangers to shark depicted in ocean scene:

oil and litter floating in water—Polluted water can harm sharks as well as other ocean life.

fishing net—Many sharks are killed when they become tangled in nets meant to catch other fish.

fishing boat from the Shark Fin Soup Company—Some fishermen kill sharks just to get their fins for a kind of soup.

resort onshore near the shark nursery—Development and the pollution that often comes with it can mean that fewer baby sharks are born in shark nurseries.

killer whale—These large predatory whales are capable of killing sharks—even ones as large as the great white shark!

Scientist for a Day
(Math)

Students estimate and count sharks and other fish in an ocean scene.

Make a copy of the reproducible on page 28 for each student. Explain to children that scientists often need to find out how many of a certain type of animal are living in an area. Ask them to imagine that they are scientists with the job of figuring out how many sharks and other fish are in the ocean scene on the reproducible.

Review the directions, making sure that students understand what an estimate is before they begin the activity. Have them fill in their estimates for both sharks and other fish before they begin counting.

Answers: In the first and third columns, answers will vary depending on students' estimates. In the second column, there are 9 sharks and 11 other fish.

Buddies or Bothers?
(Science, Art)

Students learn about relationships between sharks and other creatures.

If you were a small fish, you'd probably want to stay out of a shark's way, right? Not if you were a pilot fish. These tiny fish are in no danger of being eaten—they are too quick for a shark to catch. But they get certain perks from hanging out around sharks. For one thing, they are kept safe from other predators simply by being near the shark. After all, not many other fish want to get too close to a shark. Plus, they feed on scraps of food left over from the shark's meal. If you were a remora, you'd not only hang around a shark; you'd hang on to it! Remoras have special sticky pads on the tops of their heads that they use to cling to a shark's body.

In addition to getting a free ride, remoras also feed on parasites that grow on the shark's skin.

Not all creatures that hang around sharks are their buddies. Barnacles similar to those found on boat docks can attach to sharks' skin and grow, feeding off the shark. Copepods are tiny crustaceans that latch on to sharks' skin or even their eyes. Sometimes these copepods interfere with the shark's vision, making it difficult to see. Remoras help remove some of these bothersome shark pests.

Help your students understand the relationships between sharks and other creatures that share their world by making a bulletin board titled "Buddies or Bothers?" Cut out a large shark and place it on the bulletin board. Show students photographs or illustrations of remoras, pilot fish, copepods, and barnacles. Invite them to draw these creatures and then color and cut out their drawings. Ask kids to attach shark bothers (copepods and barnacles) onto the shark. Next, they can place shark buddies (remoras and pilot fish) on and around the shark.

Save the Sharks Campaign
(Language Arts, Science, Art)

Students educate others about sharks and encourage their protection.

Negative attitudes toward sharks discourage people from protecting them. People must learn that sharks aren't the evil killers the movies make them out to be. If this is widely known, people will be more motivated to protect sharks and their habitat. In some ways, sharks are similar to lions and tigers. They are the top predators of the sea, and they are an important link in the ocean's web of life. Now that your students have learned many fascinating things about sharks, they can teach others to respect and protect these amazing creatures.

Below are several ways for your class to launch a Save the Sharks campaign. Feel free to adapt them for your group or augment them with your ideas or those of your students.

Shark Survey—Come up with several simple questions for students to ask friends and family to determine their opinions and knowledge about sharks. Once the results are in, kids can decide which of the following activities might help people better understand sharks.

Sharks on Screen—Rent a good shark video (*Shark*, a 35-minute Eyewitness Video by Dorling Kindersley, is an excellent choice) and invite fellow students, parents, and community members to a special screening. After the movie, kids can share with the group some of the shark information they've learned. Serve shark-inspired refreshments such as shark-shaped cookies, cupcakes with paper fins on top, spreads on shark-shaped bread, and so on.

Community Displays—Check with your local library or other public place about setting up an informative shark display. The display can include shark poems and crafts from this book as well as student-made posters that contain facts about sharks, reasons that sharks need people to protect them, and colorful illustrations.

Shark Bites—Have students publish a short newspaper to distribute to fellow students and parents, containing brief articles about sharks and the dangers they face. Be sure to feature students' drawings, cartoons, and poems.

Shark Web—Create your own Web page featuring students' writing and artwork that shows what they have learned about sharks. Free step-by-step Web design help can be found at the Filamentality Web site at **www.kn.pacbell.com/wired/fil/index.html**.

Shark Party—Throw a shark theme party for fellow students, parents, and community members. Invite a shark expert from an aquarium or university to speak to your group. Have story circles in which adults or older children read books about sharks to small

groups (see Shark Resources on page 32). Serve shark-inspired refreshments (see suggestions under Sharks on Screen). And feature student posters and projects from their shark studies to educate guests about sharks.

Teaching With the "Super Sharks!" Poster

(Science, Math, Art)

Students study the poster to answer questions about sharks.

Display the "Super Sharks!" poster, and ask children the questions below. The answers appear in parentheses.

1. Which shark has been in the movies? (great white shark—from the movie *Jaws*)

2. If each shark has 5 gill slits, how many are there on all of the sharks shown? (25)

3. Which shark is the most difficult to see? (wobbegong)

4. Which shark is named after a land animal? (leopard shark)

5. Which shark is named after another ocean animal? (whale shark)

6. Which shark is shaped like a tool? (hammerhead)

7. Which shark not pictured on the poster is a class favorite? Have kids draw its picture and write its name.

The Toothy Times

(Language Arts, Math, Science)

Students read news about sharks, solve a shark puzzle, and play shark games.

Dive Into Shark News!
Give each student a copy of pages 29–31. Have students tape together the pages so that they can read it like an actual newspaper. First, read aloud the news stories on the front page. Then lead a discussion about the issues involved.

Who Caught the Fish?
In this activity students solve a shark mystery: Which shark caught the fish? First they answer questions about the size of the sharks depicted. Then they use the information to analyze the clues at the bottom of the page. Explain that they should use a process of elimination, crossing out sharks that are not the "winner." The shark that is left is the one who caught the fish.

Answers: 1—blacktip reef shark and leopard shark, 2—thresher shark, 3—cigar shark

The shark that caught the fish is the bull shark.

Shark Games

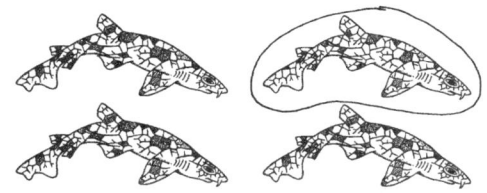

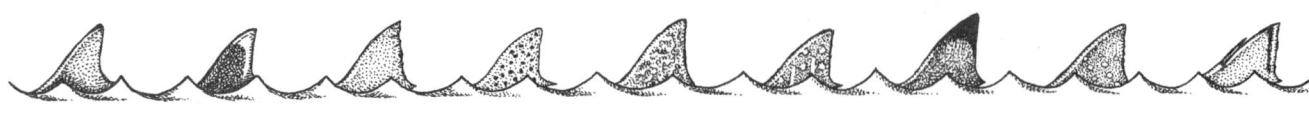

Name _____ Date _____

"Swimmin' Sharks Are We"

(to the tune of "The Addams Family")

We're toothy ocean fishes.
Other fishes taste delicious.
We are not mean; the fact is—
Swimmin' sharks are we.

Chorus:

Da da da dum—sharp teeth!
Da da da dum—eat meat!
Da da da dum. Da da da dum. Da da da dum—sharks are neat!

We don't have bones—who needs 'em?
Our skin is rough, no teasin'.
Loose tooth? Then more will squeeze in.
Swimmin' sharks are we.

Repeat chorus

We're not like in the movies.
Biting people isn't groovy.
Jaws is a bunch of hooey!
Swimmin' sharks are we.

Repeat chorus

We've swum the seas for so long.
But soon we could be all gone.
Save sharks! Please pass the word on!
Swimmin' sharks are we.

Repeat chorus

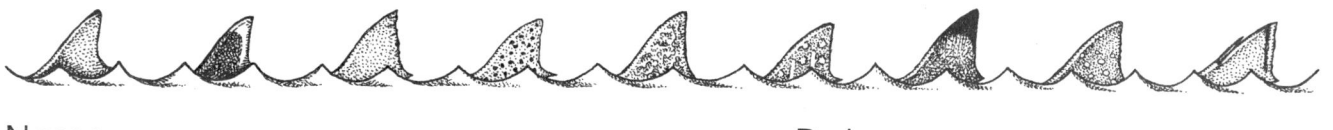

Name _____ Date _____

Make Your Own Swimmin' Shark

Cut out the fins. Then follow your teacher's directions to make a swimmin' leopard shark.

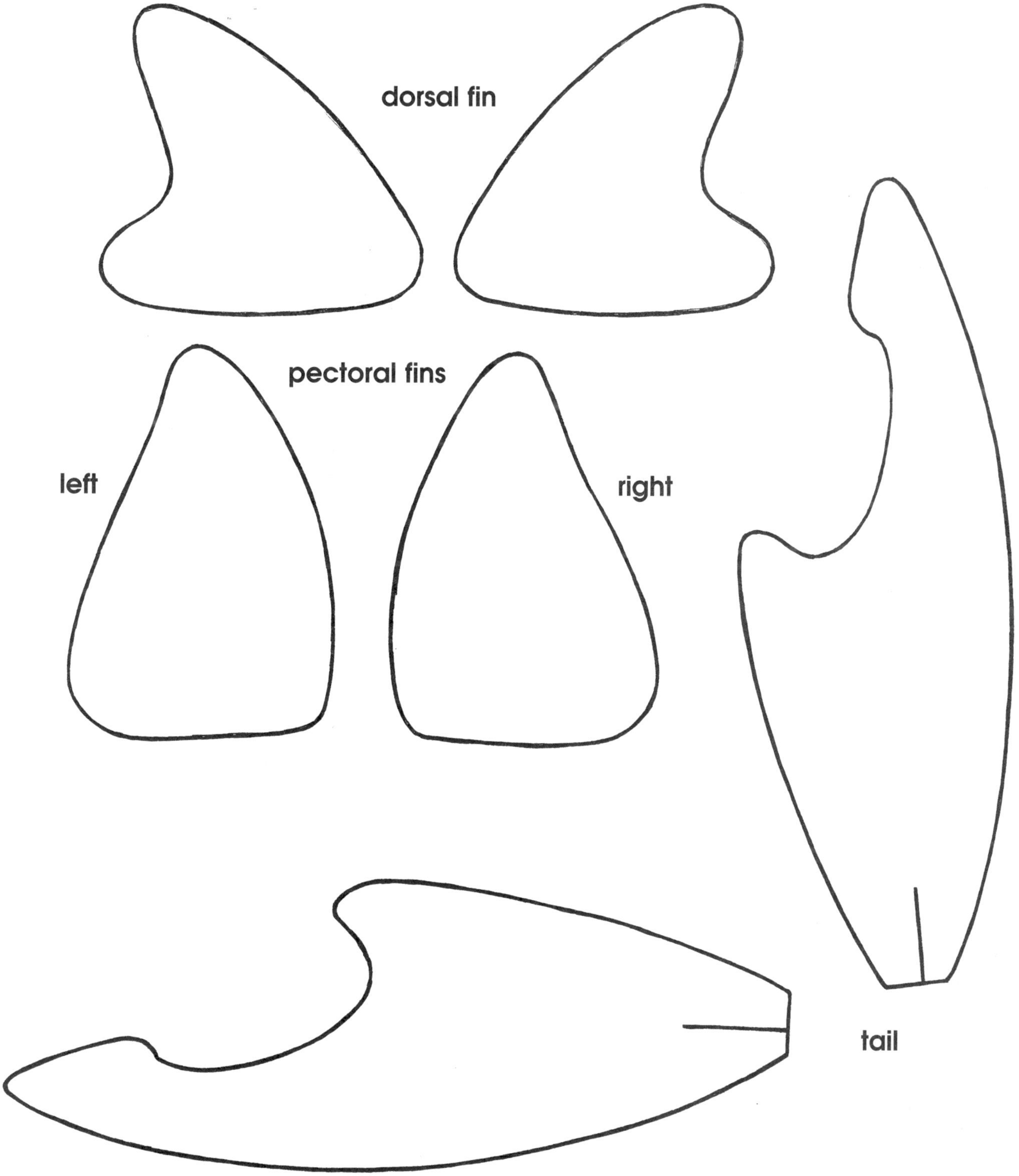

dorsal fin

pectoral fins

left   right

tail

Name _____ Date _____

What Sharp Teeth...

Read the clues below. Write the name of the shark that each clue describes. (Each name is used once.) Then color the sharks.

1. My teeth are like needles, sharp and straight.
   A fish in my mouth isn't likely to escape.
   _____

2. You wouldn't want me in the kitchen. Biscuits I don't make.
   When a fish comes close—chomp!—a round hunk of flesh I'll take.
   _____

3. My jaws are filled with jagged teeth.
   They are great for attacking creatures as big as me.
   _____

4. For me, sharp teeth wouldn't be so swell.
   I need flat teeth for crushing prey with shells.
   _____

5. I have teeth around the edges of my long, thin snout.
   If fish see my "saw" coming, they'd better watch out!
   _____

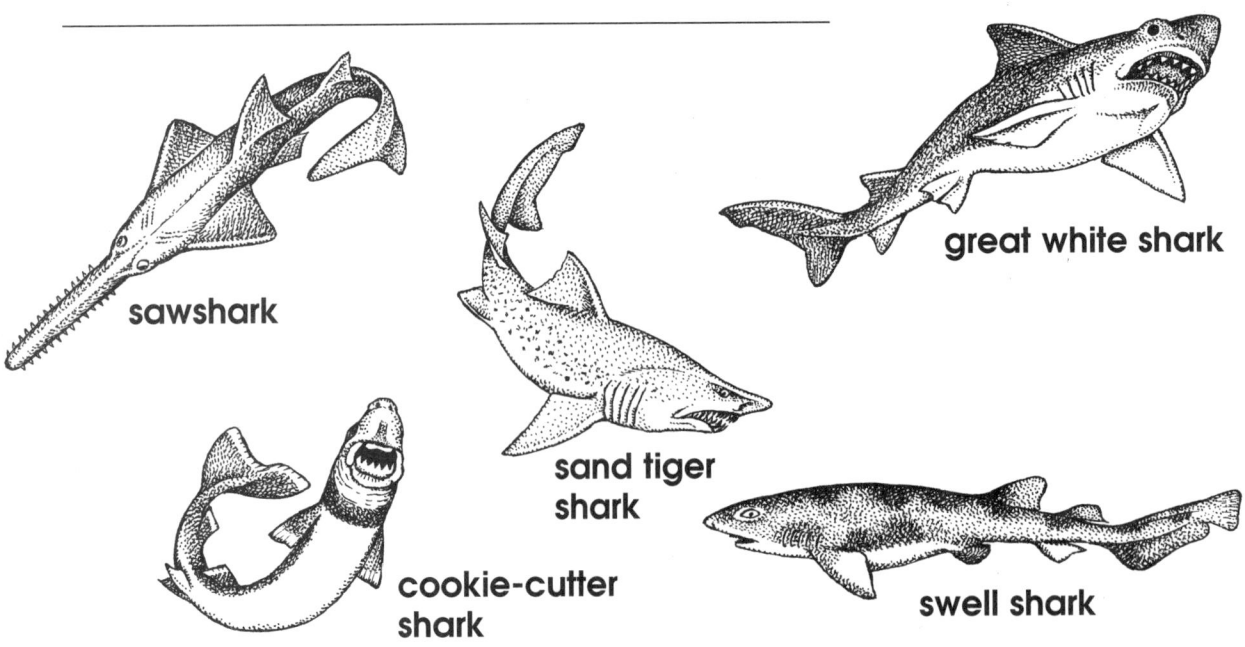

sawshark

great white shark

sand tiger shark

cookie-cutter shark

swell shark

22

Name _____   Date _____

A Nose for Hunting

Help the shark find its way through the maze! Read each question and circle the correct answer. Move through the maze from one correct answer to the next. At the end, the shark will find a treat!

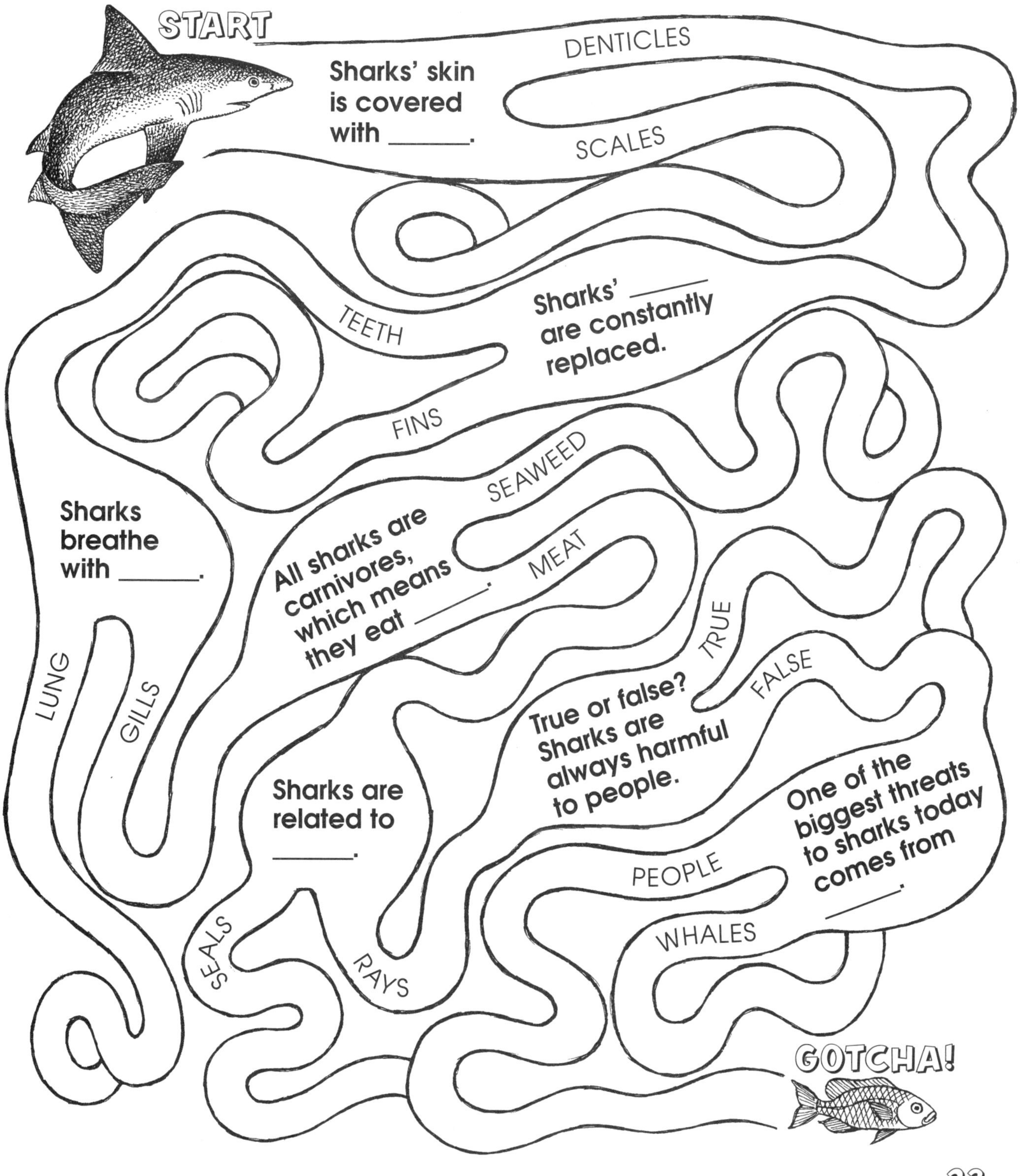

START

- Sharks' skin is covered with _____. — DENTICLES / SCALES
- Sharks' _____ are constantly replaced. — TEETH / FINS
- All sharks are carnivores, which means they eat _____. — SEAWEED / MEAT
- Sharks breathe with _____. — LUNG / GILLS
- Sharks are related to _____. — SEALS / RAYS
- True or false? Sharks are always harmful to people. — TRUE / FALSE
- One of the biggest threats to sharks today comes from _____. — PEOPLE / WHALES

GOTCHA!

23

Name _____ Date _____

The Strangest Names

Answer the questions below. Write a shark name on each line. Each name is used once.

1. Which shark "hits the nail on the head"? _____

2. Which shark can light the dark? _____

3. Which shark "wears a hat"? _____

4. Which shark is "no devil"? _____

5. Which shark is a "monster"? _____

6. Which shark is named for a striped animal? _____

hammerhead shark   **zebra shark**   **lantern shark**

angel shark

bonnethead shark

goblin shark

Make up your own shark. Draw its picture on the back of this sheet. Give your shark its own unusual name.

Name _____ Date _____

Sharks on the Move

Use the map and mileage scale to answer the question below.

Use a string to follow the shark's path. Then measure the string using the mileage scale. How many miles did the shark swim? _____

25

Name _____ Date _____

Make a Mermaid's Purse

Cut out the shapes below. Then follow your teacher's directions to make a shark egg case, called a mermaid's purse. You can use the finished project as a purse or a pouch!

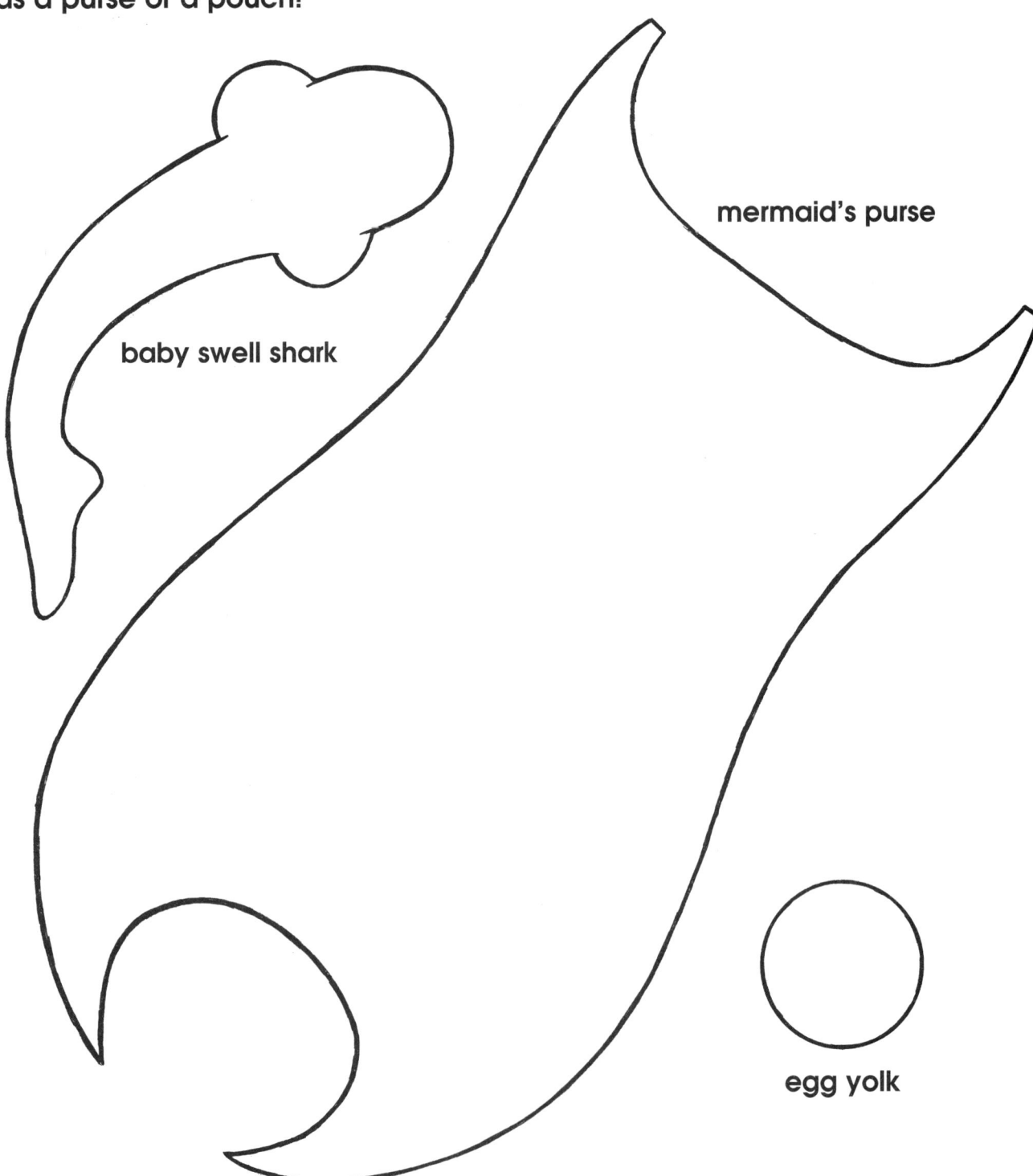

baby swell shark

mermaid's purse

egg yolk

Name _____ Date _____

Troubled Waters

Color the ocean scene below. Find and circle things that could harm the shark.

How would you help sharks? _____

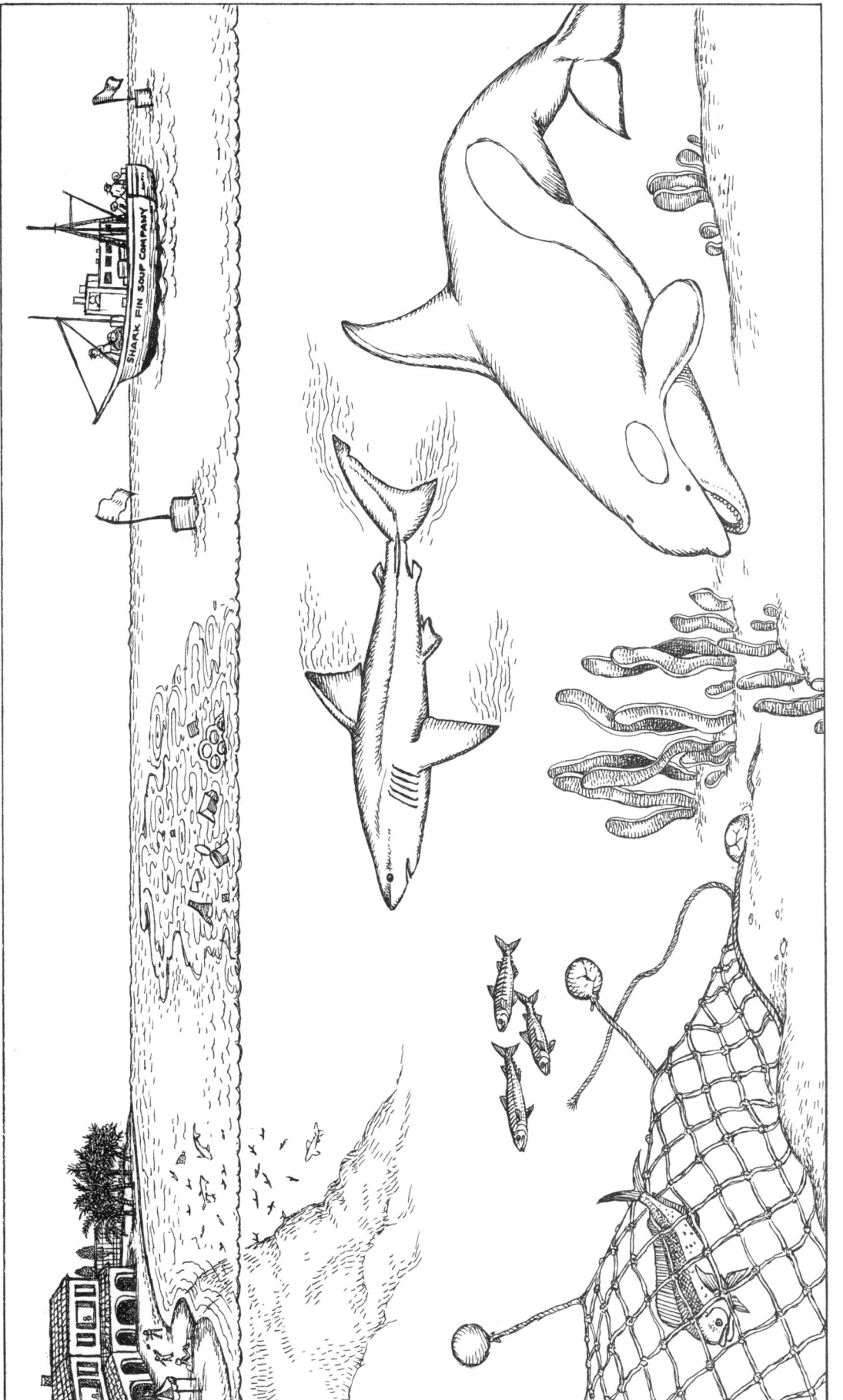

Sharks! Scholastic Professional Books

27

Name _____ Date _____

Scientist for a Day

As a scientist, your job is to count the sharks and other fish in this ocean scene. But first, can you guess how many there are of each? A guess is called an estimate. Fill in the chart below.

	Guess how many there are of each. Write your estimate.	Count and write the number.	Did you guess more or fewer than the actual number?
sharks			
other fish			

Name _____   Date _____

THE TOOTHY TIMES

Dive Into Shark News!

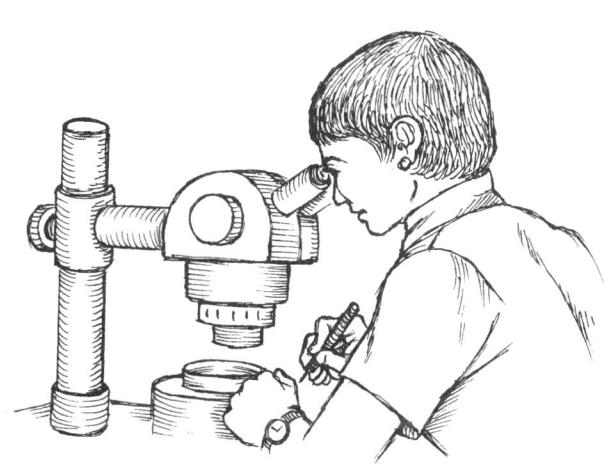

Sharks to the Rescue?

Someday sharks may save human lives! Scientists discovered that sharks rarely get cancer. The scientists wondered why and did some experiments. Even when sharks were given a substance that causes cancer, they still didn't get cancer!

Sharks are different from humans and other animals because sharks don't have bones. Their skeletons are made of cartilage. Humans have some cartilage too—in their ears, the tips of their noses, and their joints. And humans usually don't get cancer in those places.

So scientists are now studying shark cartilage. They hope it may hold the key to a cure for cancer.

Save the Sharks!

Sharks are in danger of disappearing in some places. People have been fishing for sharks for years. They have caught so many sharks that there are not many left in some places. Sharks only have a few babies at a time. These young sharks take a long time to grow up. That makes it even harder for sharks to keep their numbers up.

The government is working to protect sharks. Shark fishing is now banned in some places. And restaurant owners are trying to help, too, by not offering shark on their menus. So maybe with a little help, things will start looking up for sharks!

Name _____ Date _____

THE TOOTHY TIMES

Who Caught the Fish?

These sharks were all chasing the same fish. Which one caught it? To find out, first compare the shark sizes. Answer the questions below.

1. Which sharks are the same size? _____ and _____

2. Which shark is the biggest? _____

3. Which shark is the smallest? _____

Next, read the clues below. Cross out the sharks that did not catch fish. The one that is left is the winner!

CLUES

The winner is not the same size as another shark.

The winner is not the biggest shark.

The winner is not the smallest shark.

    blacktip reef shark

    bull shark

    thresher shark

    leopard shark

    cigar shark

The shark that caught the fish is the _____.

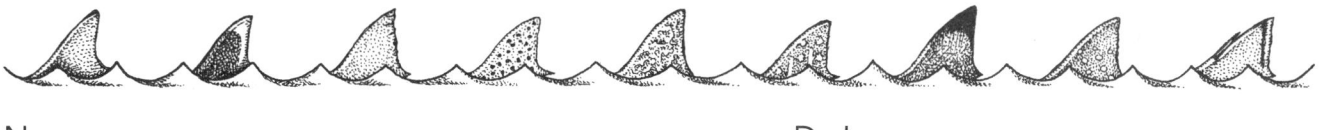

Name _____ Date _____

THE TOOTHY TIMES

Shark Games

Who's Different?

One of these sharks is not like the others. Can you spot which one and circle it?

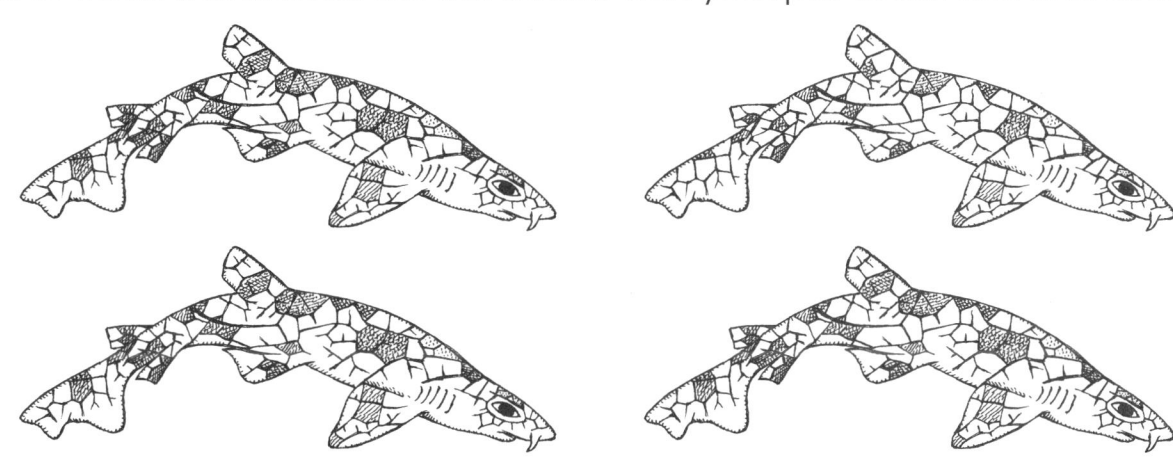

Shark Word Search

Find and circle these words.

- Denticles
- Eggs
- Fins
- Great white
- Jaws
- Leopard
- Ocean
- Sawshark
- Shark (twice)
- Swell shark
- Whale shark
- Wobbegong
- Zebra

G	W	H	A	L	E	S	H	A	R	K	Z	C
W	R	D	H	J	A	W	S	D	U	S	E	N
O	C	E	A	N	M	E	X	W	E	H	B	I
B	R	N	A	P	R	L	E	O	P	A	R	D
B	C	T	H	T	E	L	M	S	H	R	A	D
E	K	I	S	A	W	S	H	A	R	K	N	O
G	E	C	D	M	S	H	F	C	S	C	I	P
O	P	L	R	L	H	A	I	B	K	R	G	E
N	F	E	N	W	S	R	N	T	E	A	B	X
G	I	S	H	A	R	K	S	V	E	G	G	S

Shark Resources

Books for Students

Hungry, Hungry Sharks by Joanna Cole (Random House, 1986) describes various kinds of sharks in simple language.

Marine Biologist: Swimming With the Sharks by Keith Elliott Greenberg (Blackbirch Press, 1996) describes the real-life experiences of a shark researcher.

Outside and Inside Sharks by Sandra Markle (Atheneum Books for Young Readers, 1996) lets kids peek inside a shark's body to see what makes it tick. Other close-ups focus on shark skin, teeth, and ears.

Questions and Answers About Sharks by Ann McGovern (Scholastic, 1995) is a comprehensive yet brief look at sharks and their world.

Shark in the Sea by Joanne Ryder (Morrow Junior Books, 1997) tells an imaginative story about a boy changing into a shark.

Sharks by Russell Freedman (Holiday House, 1985) provides lively information about different kinds of sharks.

Sharks by Seymour Simon (HarperCollins, 1995) contains intriguing photographs and information about sharks.

The World of Sharks by Andrew Langley (Bookwright Press, 1988) is written for older students but features interesting photographs.

Books for Teachers

The Encyclopedia of Sharks by Steve and Jane Parker (Firefly, 1999) provides a solid and informative introduction to sharks, filled with facts, illustrations, maps, and diagrams. Children will also enjoy the intriguing photographs.

The Shark Almanac by Thomas B. Allen (Lyons Press, 1999) is a comprehensive overview that dispels myths and covers more than 100 shark species, as well as shark folklore, current research, conservation efforts, and more. Includes illustrations and photographs.

Sharks edited by J. D. Stevens (Checkmark Books, 1999) is a lively and informative resource covering a wide range of topics and including over 300 spectacular photographs.

Classroom Resources

Eyewitness: Shark by Miranda MacQuitty (Knopf, 1992) presents a compelling resource book for kids using text, photos, illustrations, maps, and 3-D models.

Shark is a 35-minute Eyewitness Video by Dorling Kindersley, 1994.

Sharks (Reader's Digest, 1998) is a book featuring descriptions of many shark species.

"Under Attack" is an interesting article that appeared in the September 19, 1997 issue of *Time for Kids*.

Web Sites

The Discovery Channel's Web site includes a page devoted to sharks. The "Shark Zone" features a virtual shark tank, shark cam, and an "interview" with a shark. Visit **www.discovery.com** and enter "sharks" as a search keyword.

Shark Friends is a site for students and teachers. It includes information about sharks and other marine animals, as well as games and activities. Visit **www.sharkfriends.com**.

Think Quest provides a list of sites devoted to sharks. Go to **www.thinkquest.org/library** and search for "sharks."

At **The JASON Project Web Site**, search for "sharks" to find more than 50 articles and activities. The site is at **www.jasonproject.org**.